Original title:
Nostalgic Notion

Copyright © 2024 Creative Arts Management OÜ
All rights reserved.

Author: Christian Leclair
ISBN HARDBACK: 978-9916-90-700-9
ISBN PAPERBACK: 978-9916-90-701-6

Mementos of Heartfelt Goodbyes

In every smile, a memory stays,
A whisper of laughter, the light of our days.
Though the time has come, and roads must part,
These moments we shared, engraved in my heart.

With every tear, a lesson learned,
In the fires of friendship, our souls have burned.
Though miles may stretch, and shadows grow long,
Our bond will remain, forever strong.

In the silence that falls, I hear your voice,
Reminding me gently, we had no choice.
The warmth of your hug, the stories we spun,
In the tapestry woven, we are still one.

So here's to the nights, to dreams yet to chase,
To the laughter and love, in our sacred space.
With every farewell, a promise is made,
In the mementos of life, we'll never fade.

Recollections in a Whispering Breeze

In the hush of twilight's glow,
Memories dance, soft and slow.
Each whisper a tale, cleverly spun,
Echoes of laughter, when days were fun.

Leaves rustle gently in the night,
Carrying dreams into the light.
Moments once lost, now find their way,
In the breeze, they long to stay.

Harmonies of Hallowed Time

Notes of the past in every chime,
Resonate deeply through hallowed time.
A symphony playing within the heart,
Binding the old with the new, a sweet art.

Like whispered prayers in the stillness found,
Each moment's echo in layers unbound.
With each heartbeat, a rhythm remains,
Melodies linger, wrapped in refrains.

The Canvas of a Whimsical Past

Strokes of color on memories' page,
A whimsical tale of youthful age.
Dreams intertwine with laughter's hue,
Moments painted in shades so true.

Brushes of joy in sunlight's embrace,
Capture the essence of time and space.
Each canvas whispers secrets untold,
Stories of love in colors bold.

The Sail of Sentiment's Vessel

On waves of feeling, we gently glide,
With the sail of sentiment, we ride.
Each gust a memory, fresh and bright,
Guiding us forward into the night.

Anchors of longing seek the shore,
Whispers of love that we can't ignore.
With every tide, the heart expands,
Sailing through time, held in gentle hands.

A Canvas of Worn-out Wishes

Brush strokes of time, they fade away,
Hopes once vibrant, now muted and gray.
Promises linger, like shadows in light,
A canvas of dreams, lost out of sight.

Each wish a thread, frayed at the seam,
Tangled in silence, caught in a dream.
Fates intertwine, then softly unspool,
Life paints the picture, a haunting jewel.

Fragments of laughter, whispers of tears,
Echoes of longing through all the years.
What once was bold, now delicately drawn,
Awaits the dawn of a brighter tomorrow.

Yet in the silence, a glimmer remains,
A spark of hope that still softly gains.
Though worn-out wishes may drift with the tide,
In the heart's deep canvas, they still abide.

Whispers of a Bygone Era

Faded voices drift in the air,
Carried by echoes of memories rare.
Stories untold in the rustling leaves,
A tapestry woven, yet time deceives.

Moments enshrined, like dust in the sun,
Laughter and sorrow, two hearts come undone.
Every fleeting glance, a tale to be spun,
Whispers of history, they linger and run.

Chasing the shadows of footsteps once known,
In the embrace of the past, we're never alone.
Time stretches thin, like a spider's silk thread,
Each whisper an echo of words left unsaid.

Yet in the silence, we still find the glow,
Of dreams that were born in a world we once know.
The whispers survive, as they softly confide,
In the heart's quiet chamber, the past will abide.

Echoes of Yesterday's Dreams

In the twilight hour, the echoes resound,
Memories flutter, no longer unbound.
Dreams of the past, like leaves in the breeze,
Dance through the darkness, yearning to please.

Fleeting possessions we held oh so dear,
Whispers of laughter now tinged with a tear.
Each moment a flicker, a spark in the night,
Echoes of dreams that still chase the light.

Winds of remembrance through soft meadows roam,
Guiding our hearts as they long for a home.
Time may erase what we think we have lost,
Yet memories linger, no matter the cost.

In quiet reflection, the shadows retain,
The warmth of the dreams that defy all the pain.
Though yesterday's echoes may fade and depart,
They linger forever, engraved on the heart.

Faded Photographs of Time

Dusty old albums, with pictures to see,
Faded reminders of who we can be.
Moments forever captured in frame,
Each photograph whispers a bittersweet name.

Sunlight spilled softly on days filled with cheer,
Frozen in time, yet distant and near.
Laughter and sorrow, interwoven in hue,
Memories linger, both cherished and blue.

Ghosts in the images, smiles in repose,
Tell tales of love that the heart still knows.
Every torn edge bears a story untold,
In each faded moment, a treasure of gold.

Through the lens of the past, we gaze and we sigh,
For moments now gone that we once held high.
Faded photographs breathe remnants of grace,
A journey remembered, time's gentle embrace.

Bottle Caps and Beloved Games

In the sunlit yard we played,
Bottle caps scattered, plans laid.
Each toss a treasure, laughter bright,
In the echoes of childhood delight.

We raced to the finish, hearts in sync,
With every cheer, we dared to think.
Games of the past, our spirits soared,
In memories cherished, joy restored.

Those golden days, so carefree,
Captured moments, just you and me.
Countless smiles, in breeze's sway,
In bottle caps, forever we play.

Time may change us, but we'll remain,
Two souls connected, through joy and pain.
In the laughter, the games we claim,
Will always spark the gentle flame.

Lanterns in a Gray Twilight

Lanterns glow in fading light,
Whispers dance in the gentle night.
Shadows stretch on cobbled streets,
As heartbeats echo, softly meet.

In corners dim, soft stories told,
Memories draped in hues of gold.
The twilight whispers secrets deep,
In dreams we wander, while shadows creep.

With every flicker, hope ignites,
In lanterns bright, through endless nights.
We gather warmth, we search and find,
In the gray twilight, love is blind.

Embers fade, yet still we stay,
Chasing stars that guide our way.
Together here, we'll always be,
In lanterns' glow, forever free.

The Craft of Remembering

In the whispers of the past,
Memories weave, a spell that's cast.
Threads of laughter, joy, and pain,
In the fabric of life, we gain.

Every moment, a stitch of grace,
In the quilt of time, we find our place.
Crafted memories, vivid and dear,
In the craft of remembering, we steer.

From faded photos to tales retold,
In the warmth of hearts, our lives unfold.
Through bittersweet, we navigate,
In threads of love, we celebrate.

Gathered close, in silent prayer,
Remembering those who linger there.
In the craft of life, we choose to treasure,
Each moment a gift, beyond all measure.

Unraveled Yarns of Togetherness

With every twist, our stories bind,
Unraveled yarns, the threads we find.
In colors bright and edges worn,
We weave our tales, together born.

Through laughter shared and tears well spent,
In every knot, our hearts are lent.
Each stitch a memory, soft embrace,
In the tapestry of our shared space.

We travel far through fabric's grace,
Together we stitch, no time to waste.
In the warmth of hands that hold so tight,
Our unraveled yarns take flight in light.

In every loop, a promise made,
In every hue, our love displayed.
Forever woven, our stories claim,
Unraveled yarns, in love's sweet name.

Gardens of Lost Relationships

In gardens where laughter used to bloom,
Amidst the weeds, fond memories loom.
Faded petals on the ground,
Silent echoes, no longer found.

Time has wilted each sweet embrace,
Leaving only a hollow space.
Once vibrant colors turned to grey,
As love's fragrance fades away.

Nostalgia's Golden Hour

Golden sun, the evening's embrace,
Whispers of youth in this sacred space.
Flickering shadows dance on the wall,
Recalling moments that rise and fall.

Laughter lingers like warm summer breeze,
Painting the past with delicate ease.
Each heartbeat a story left untold,
In the sunset's light, memories unfold.

Chasing Shadows of Old Adventures

Beneath the oak where we carved our dreams,
Lost in stories, or so it seems.
Adventures once bold now fade with time,
Leaving behind a whispered rhyme.

We chased the stars 'til the break of dawn,
While the world was sleeping, we carried on.
Yet shadows linger where we used to roam,
In the twilight, they guide us home.

The Nest of Faded Dreams

In the attic where old hopes reside,
Once woven tightly, now set aside.
Dusty corners hold fragments of care,
Each thread unraveled, still hanging there.

Dreams like feathers, soft and light,
Whisper secrets in the dead of night.
In this nest of what could have been,
I find solace, through loss I glean.

Echoes of Yesteryear

In the stillness of night, they roam,
Footfalls trace paths once known.
Memories drift like soft smoke,
Whispers of secrets long woke.

Ghostly laughter dances on air,
A melody of love, despair.
Faint shadows play on the wall,
Remnants of a life, so small.

In the corners of my mind,
Old faces are intertwined.
Time has a way to enthrall,
Echoing through the silent hall.

To cherish the moments we find,
A tapestry woven, intertwined.
The past holds treasures we seek,
In echoes, our hearts softly speak.

Reverie of Forgotten Dreams

In a garden where shadows fall,
Softly blooms the faded thrall.
Petals whisper tales of the night,
Where hopes once soared, now take flight.

Beneath the stars, wishes drift,
Carried by the moon's soft lift.
Each heartbeat a silent sigh,
As dreams of yore flutter by.

Time has a way to erase,
The vivid hues of hope's embrace.
Yet in the twilight, they gleam,
Shadows conjure lost esteem.

Awake, I hold onto the gleams,
Forever caught in these dreams.
The night whispers of what could be,
In reveries, I am set free.

Whispers from the Attic

In the attic, dust motes dance,
Old wood creaks before the chance.
Forgotten toys and garments old,
Stories of lives silently told.

Through cobwebs thick, memories weave,
Messages from those who believe.
Faded letters, yellowed and torn,
Echoes of love, memories worn.

A trunk holds treasures so dear,
Sealed with laughter, wrapped in fear.
Each item a portal, a gate,
To lives that linger, to celebrate.

Whispers of the past intertwine,
A tapestry worn but divine.
In echoes of time, we find our way,
Through whispers that never decay.

The Color of Old Photographs

Faded sepia tones unfold,
Stories captured, memories old.
In frames of time, lives appear,
Moments cherished, crystal clear.

Each image whispers of laughter,
A snapshot of what comes after.
When eyes sparkled with delight,
And hearts soared into the night.

Grass underfoot, skies so blue,
The warmth of days we once knew.
Light creeping in, chairs set for two,
Forever caught in that view.

The color of memories remains,
In every joy, in every pain.
Old photographs tell a tale,
Of love's journey, of winds that sail.

Flashes of Childhood Gleams

In the garden, laughter rings,
Chasing shadows, chasing dreams.
Kites flying high, beneath the sun,
Childhood whispers, never done.

Splash of colors, paint the sky,
Running free, letting hearts fly.
Moments captured, fleeting bliss,
Innocence wrapped in a sweet kiss.

Timeworn Trails of Thought

Footprints faded in the sand,
Echoes of a guiding hand.
Winding paths through fields of gold,
Stories waiting to be told.

Whispers linger in the breeze,
Rustling leaves, a gentle tease.
Memories dance like fireflies,
In the dusk, beneath the skies.

Letters from the Past

Yellowed pages, ink still bright,
Words of comfort, fading light.
Promises made in whispered tones,
A treasure trove of heart's own stones.

In each letter, a love once shared,
Heartfelt wishes, gently bared.
Time may fade, but truth remains,
In every line, the joy, the pains.

Reflections in Dusty Mirrors

Glimmers caught in specks of dust,
Truths hidden beneath the rust.
Fractured images of who we were,
Echoes of the dreams that stir.

Wipe the glass, see clearer days,
Memories lost in a smoky haze.
Each reflection tells a tale,
Of hopes and fears we still unveil.

Timeworn Melodies

In twilight's glow, the echoes call,
Soft whispers dance as shadows fall.
Notes of the past, like leaves, they sway,
Fading memories, dreams led astray.

Each chord a story, sweet and bittersweet,
A melody lost, a heart's swift beat.
Timeworn songs in the silent air,
Drawing us back to moments rare.

Shadows of Summers Past

Beneath the tree where laughter bloomed,
Sun-kissed days in light consumed.
Butterflies flit on golden light,
Memories dance, both bold and bright.

Now shadows linger, silent and deep,
Echoes of joy in the heart they keep.
Seasons turn, yet still we yearn,
For summers lost, as candles burn.

Haunting Memories in Dusk's Embrace

Dusk wraps around like a soft, warm shawl,
Whispers of bygone days softly call.
Flickering lights in the fading sky,
Ghosts of the past gently drift by.

In every sigh, a story unfolds,
A tapestry woven with threads of gold.
Time's gentle hand steals moments sweet,
Yet in our hearts, their rhythm repeats.

Faded Pages of Innocence

In a dusty book, the pages lie,
Stories of youth that softly sigh.
Each word a treasure, now worn with age,
Tales of laughter on life's grand stage.

With every turn, nostalgia flows,
Ink-stained dreams where innocence grows.
Though years have passed, the spirit stays,
In faded pages, love always plays.

The Dance of Remembered Hearts

In twilight's glow, we find our steps,
The whispers soft, where memory wept.
A gentle sway, the shadows play,
In echoes of love, we'll drift away.

A melody flows through the silent air,
Each heartbeat sings of moments rare.
With every glance, a story shared,
Two souls entwined, forever paired.

The flicker of flames in a starlit night,
Reminds us of passion, pure and bright.
And as we turn in this waltz so grand,
The dance of remembered hearts, hand in hand.

Pages of an Unwritten History

Blank pages wait, a story untold,
With ink of dreams and visions bold.
A canvas anew, the pen in hand,
To shape the future, to understand.

Each moment sparks, a chance to write,
In the depth of day, or the hush of night.
The whispers of life, in echoes resound,
Unlocking the truths yet to be found.

With every stroke, our voices arise,
The heartbeats sync with the universe's sighs.
Together we weave, with hopes that soar,
Pages of history, forever more.

The Sweetness of Lingering Melancholy

Beneath the rain, soft tears descend,
Whispers of loss, but time can mend.
In shadows cast, a tender grace,
The sweetness found in each embrace.

Gentle sighs that fill the air,
Memories linger, too precious to bear.
Each fleeting moment, a bittersweet song,
In the heart's deep chambers, where we belong.

Yet from the ache, beauty we glean,
In every shadow, a soft, silver sheen.
For in the sorrow, love's echo plays,
The sweetness of life in its deepest ways.

A Patchwork of Cherished Tales

In fragments bright, our stories dwell,
Each thread a memory, a spell to tell.
A quilt of laughter, woven tight,
In patchwork dreams that dance in the light.

From childhood whispers to starlit nights,
These cherished tales bring heart's delights.
With every stitch, the past unfolds,
A tapestry rich in colors bold.

Through trials faced and joys embraced,
In this woven world, love interlaced.
Together we share, as seasons change,
A patchwork of life, forever strange.

A Chronicle of Fleeting Joys

In gardens where the sunlight plays,
Laughter dances on bright summer days.
Children's whispers carried by the breeze,
Moments cherished, like leaves on trees.

A fleeting glance, a touch so light,
Warmth of friendships, souls taking flight.
A fleeting joy, a spark of delight,
Fading softly into the night.

A melody sung in soft twilight,
Dreams weave together, hearts ignite.
In those small joys, we find our way,
Mapping out our bright, vibrant days.

Yet time moves on, like a gentle stream,
Leaving behind the sweetest dream.
A chronicle written in smiles and sighs,
An echo of laughter that never dies.

The Silence Between Old Friends

In quiet corners where memories dwell,
Silence speaks louder than words can tell.
Old friends sit with easy grace,
Each silence a warmth, a familiar place.

Eyes share stories of years long past,
Friendship's bond, a spell that's cast.
No need for chatter, no restless sighs,
In stillness, the heart truly replies.

A knowing smile, a gentle nod,
Together in silence, where paths have trod.
Time stands still in this sacred space,
The history shared, a comforting trace.

In moments of quiet, life's truths unfold,
In the silence, we need not be told.
For the love that binds, no words can confine,
In the silence, a heartbeat, our souls align.

Vintage Shadows of Heartfelt Bonds

Footsteps echo on cobblestone lanes,
Whispers of love, where memory remains.
Vintage shadows of moments we share,
Threading through time, a tapestry rare.

A photograph fading in sun's embrace,
Captured smiles in a fragile space.
Each bond, a story etched in time's mold,
Heartfelt treasures, more precious than gold.

As seasons change and years slip by,
The essence of friendship will not die.
In the shadows, the heart finds its song,
Reminding us all where we belong.

With every laugh and every tear,
We weave our stories, crystal clear.
Through vintage shadows, our hearts will blend,
In the gallery of life, love has no end.

The Canvas of Time: Colors Revisited

Brushstrokes of moments, vivid and bright,
A canvas of time in morning light.
Colors revisited, old yet anew,
Painting the heart with shades of you.

Each hue a memory, each tone a dream,
Waves of laughter, soft as a stream.
Time holds the palette, rich with the past,
In each stroke of love, forever will last.

With splashes of joy and tints of regret,
The canvas expands, but we don't forget.
Each moment captured, a piece of the heart,
In the art of living, we play our part.

As the colors blend and shift with the light,
Time leads us forward into the night.
Yet in our creation, a promise we keep,
A lasting masterpiece, our hearts shall reap.

Portraits of Yesterday's Joy

In frames of gold with laughter bright,
Old photos whisper stories light.
Each smile a moment, forever caught,
In echoes of days that time forgot.

Children played, their laughter so free,
Under the shade of the old oak tree.
Memories dance on the edges of time,
In the gallery of heart, they brightly shine.

Old toys sit silent, lost in the dust,
Yet they hold secrets, in them we trust.
With every glance, a memory to keep,
In portraits of joy, our hearts take a leap.

So here we stand, tracing the past,
In every picture, a shadow is cast.
The joy of yesterday, forever near,
In moments we treasure, we hold dear.

Serenades from a Timeless Past

Soft melodies float through the air,
Whispers of love, of longing and care.
Guitar strings strum the heart's gentle plea,
In warm, dusky light, souls dance free.

Old records spin with a crackle and glide,
Songs of an era where passions abide.
Each note a thread in the fabric of time,
Weaving together both heart and rhyme.

In candlelight flickers, romance can bloom,
As shadows from yesteryear fill the room.
Voices like silk wrap us in embrace,
With serenades sweet, we find our place.

The tunes may fade, but the feeling remains,
In every heartbeat, still softly sustains.
For in melodies true, we often find,
A timeless connection that binds heart and mind.

The Umbrella of Shared Moments

Beneath the wide arch of gray clouds,
We share a laugh, lost in the crowds.
Raindrops gather on the fabric soft,
Each droplet sings of moments aloft.

Holding on tight, we weather the storm,
In the shelter of love, feeling so warm.
A dance in the rain, as the world spins 'round,
With each fleeting heartbeat, joy is found.

Colors of life weave through the skies,
Like a tapestry bright, where hope never dies.
The umbrella shields us from all that we face,
In shared moments cherished, we find our place.

So let the thunder roar, let the winds play,
For together we flourish, come what may.
With laughter and love, we'll weather the day,
Under the umbrella, come sunshine or gray.

Breaths of Antiquity

In the walls of the old, stories reside,
Whispers of ancients who once took pride.
Dust of the ages floats softly around,
In breaths of antiquity, wisdom is found.

Echoes of footsteps, time's gentle trace,
In every corner, the past leaves its grace.
The silence sings loudly, memories flare,
In the heart of the old, we taste the air.

Candles flicker, shadows waltz by,
As centuries linger, they softly sigh.
Each crack in the walls holds a tale to share,
In the stillness of time, we breathe in the rare.

A window to yesteryear's gentle embrace,
In breaths of antiquity, we find our place.
For through every moment that time dares to steal,
The spirit of life is forever real.

Crimson Leaves of Change

In the whispering winds of fall,
Crimson leaves begin to call.
Shimmering gold and rust embrace,
Nature dons her vibrant face.

Underneath a canopy bright,
The world transforms with sheer delight.
Gentle breezes dance and twirl,
Spinning dreams in a twinkling swirl.

Each leaf carries a tale untold,
Of summer's warmth, now fading gold.
Transitions mold our tender hearts,
As nature plays her shifting parts.

In the quiet, change appears,
Whispering softly through our years.
Embrace the colors, let them thrive,
For in their breath, we feel alive.

The Embrace of Yesteryear's Dawn

Sunrise spills its golden hue,
Awakening memories anew.
Echoes linger, soft and clear,
The dawn of yesteryears draws near.

In quiet corners of the mind,
Fragments of joy we often find.
Laughter dances on the breeze,
Whispers of love like springtime trees.

Time may fade, yet hearts hold tight,
To cherished moments, pure delight.
Each sunrise brings a chance to see,
The beauty in our history.

Embrace the shadows, kiss the light,
In every dawn, let's take flight.
For yesteryear, though far away,
Shapes who we are in every way.

Fading Footprints on the Sand

Along the shore where waves do meet,
Footprints linger, soft and sweet.
With every tide, they ebb and flow,
Stories written in sand below.

Each step taken, in fleeting grace,
A moment etched in time and space.
Yet as the sea embraces land,
Our memories shift like grains of sand.

The sun sets low, a gentle sigh,
Where daylight fades, the shadows lie.
Though footprints fade under the tide,
In hearts, their beauty won't subside.

So let the waves wash them away,
Embracing change with night and day.
For every mark, a tale we weave,
In the sands of time, we truly believe.

Worn Quilts of Warm Memories

Threads of laughter stitched with care,
Worn quilts wrap us, love laid bare.
In colors bright and patterns dear,
They tell of moments held near.

Faded patches, each a tale,
Of sunny days and gentle trails.
Every fold a heartbeat's song,
In a tapestry where we belong.

Shared whispers on a winter night,
The warmth of kin, a deep delight.
A gentle hug in every seam,
Worn quilts hold our sweetest dreams.

As seasons shift and years unwind,
These memories, forever kind.
In every stitch, a loving trace,
Of time spent well, a warm embrace.

Windows to Remembered Days

Through glass panes soft and clear,
I gaze upon the past so dear.
Sunlight dances, shadows play,
A tapestry of yesterday.

Dusty corners hold their secrets,
Whispers of joys and regrets.
Each moment framed with care,
In their glow, I'm always there.

The world outside may shift and change,
Yet this view, it feels so strange.
Familiar faces in the light,
Drawn forth from the endless night.

As seasons turn and moments fade,
These windows keep the memories made.
A glimpse of love, a brief embrace,
In every sigh, I find my place.

Shadows of Long-lost Laughter

Echoes linger in the air,
Fleeting giggles, memories rare.
Silhouettes dance, both near and far,
Faded joy beneath a star.

Once we played beneath the sun,
Chasing dreams, we'd always run.
Now the nights stretch long and wide,
Where laughter once would softly glide.

In quiet corners, silence reigns,
Nostalgia flows through hidden veins.
Each shadow holds a whispered tale,
Of laughter's rise, of joy's soft sail.

Yet in the stillness, hope remains,
For every heart that love attains.
With every heartbeat, we still find,
A trace of joy that's intertwined.

Fragments of a Lost Melody

Notes are scattered on the breeze,
Whispers of songs that still can tease.
Echoes of what once was whole,
Fragments touch the aching soul.

Strings of laughter, keys of sorrow,
Fleeting dreams of a bright tomorrow.
In every pause and lingering chord,
Memories rest, gently stored.

As evening falls, the silence swells,
In tiny hearts, a story dwells.
Each fragment calls, a soft refrain,
A melody of joy and pain.

Yet through the night, hope persists,
The music of life cannot be missed.
In every heartbeat, tune shall sway,
Fragments weave a bright ballet.

Rewound Memories

In the attic of my mind,
Dusty tapes and thoughts entwined.
Playbacks of when time stood still,
Rewound moments, memories thrill.

Faded pictures of laughter's glow,
Chasing sunlight, letting go.
Each rewind brings back the light,
Embracing shadows of the night.

With every flicker, I recall,
The echoes of a wistful call.
Scenes replay with a tender grace,
In this sacred, timeless space.

Though years may pass and seasons change,
These rewound threads remain in range.
For in the heart, they find their way,
To guide my steps, come what may.

The Cradle of Yesteryears

In shadows deep, the echoes play,
Of laughter light, a sweet ballet.
Where time stood still, in quiet grace,
Each whisper tells a tender space.

The gentle rock of dreams once shared,
On softest clouds, our hopes declared.
In every sigh, a story blooms,
The warmth of love, in silent rooms.

The world beyond, in twilight's glow,
Reflects the warmth of hearts we know.
The cradle rocks with memories near,
Each precious moment held so dear.

Through polished woods, the years glide by,
A fleeting glimpse of days gone by.
Yet in this space, we shall remain,
In sweet embrace, where love sustains.

Hues of Remembrance

The sunset splashes, gold and red,
With every hue, a thought is fed.
In moments lost, the colors swell,
Echoes soft, where memories dwell.

The shades of joy, the tones of pain,
In every brush, a heartfelt gain.
The canvas speaks of life's embrace,
In vibrant strokes, our past we trace.

A silken thread in twilight's hand,
We weave our dreams, like grains of sand.
Each whispered shade, a tale unfurls,
A tapestry of all our worlds.

With every brush, a tear, a laugh,
The hues of time, our humble craft.
In colors bold, or soft, serene,
Remembrance blooms, a timeless scene.

Threads of an Old Tapestry

In faded cloth, the stories wove,
Of distant lands we used to rove.
Each thread entwined, a path well-tread,
Recalling warmth where once we fed.

A needle's dance through time and tears,
Stitches carved by joy and fears.
In every mark, a heart's intent,
The fabric hums with love well-spent.

The colors clash, then softly blend,
A masterpiece that has no end.
In woven knots, our lives are bound,
The finest tales in fibers found.

So gather 'round this tapestry,
And let its threads set spirits free.
For in each weave, our essence lives,
A legacy that always gives.

The Distant Hum of Familiar Tunes

Across the fields, a melody flows,
In gentle waves, where sunlight glows.
A distant hum, a song of yore,
It stirs the heart, and calls for more.

In whispers soft, the notes entwine,
Of cherished days, when love was fine.
Each sound a whisper from the past,
A fleeting echo, unsurpassed.

As twilight drapes the world in blue,
The familiar tune brings forth the true.
In softest sighs, we hear the song,
A symphony where we belong.

So close your eyes, let music soar,
Embrace the warmth of what's in store.
For in each hum, a memory streams,
A gentle balm for all our dreams.

Ghosts of Forgotten Summers

Whispers of laughter in the breeze,
Faded echoes beneath the trees.
Sun-kissed days now lost in dreams,
Memories linger, torn at the seams.

Footsteps wander on paths of gold,
Stories of love and secrets untold.
Time paints the air with a gentle sigh,
Ghosts of summers drift gently by.

The warmth of sun upon our skin,
Golden moments where we begin.
Yet shadows dance in the twilight glow,
Haunting the hearts of those we know.

In the twilight, we find our way,
Through forgotten summers, we long to stay.
With every shadow that passes near,
We embrace the memories, dear and clear.

The Sweet Scent of Old Books

Pages whisper stories from the past,
In the quiet, their secrets cast.
The sweet scent of paper, worn and grey,
Takes us back to a simpler day.

Ink-stained dreams on a faded page,
Transport us to a different age.
Each chapter holds a world to explore,
Each line beckons for so much more.

Time is captured, a moment's embrace,
In the silence, we find our place.
Lost in the tales that draw us in,
The sweet scent of old books, where we begin.

With every turn, we write our fate,
In the heart of stories, we resonate.
And though the world outside may stray,
The sweet scent of old books leads the way.

Tides of Time's Embrace

Waves crash softly on the shore,
Whispers of time that we explore.
The tide pulls back, revealing sand,
Memories slip like grains through hand.

In the ebb and flow of life's great sea,
Moments fade but never flee.
Each tide a tale, untold, unbroken,
The breaths of time, we stand unspoken.

Soft sunsets that paint the sky,
Remind us of days that swiftly fly.
As the ocean sings a lullaby,
Tides of time's embrace draw us nigh.

In the stillness, we feel so small,
Yet time's caress enfolds us all.
With every wave, we find our grace,
Lost in the tides of time's embrace.

Moonlit Memories

Under stars, we shared our dreams,
In the glow of night, soft and keen.
Moonlight bathes the world in silver,
Memories twirl, forever to shiver.

Whispers float on the evening air,
Promises spoken, without a care.
In the darkness, hearts intertwined,
Moonlit memories, forever enshrined.

Each moment captured in a glance,
Lost in the magic of a fleeting chance.
As shadows dance, we softly sway,
Beneath the moonlight, we drift away.

In memory's arms, we always find,
The gentle echoes of heart and mind.
Forever cherished, we hold them tight,
In the sweet embrace of the soft moonlight.

The Lure of Yesterday's Horizon

Beneath the sky in shades of gold,
Whispers of dreams from days of old.
The sun dips low, a spark ignites,
Painting memories in fading lights.

Waves of time crash on the shore,
Echoes of laughter, tales of yore.
Chasing shadows, we roam along,
In every heartbeat, a forgotten song.

Horizon beckons, softly it calls,
Promises linger like painted walls.
With every step, a story unfolds,
In the lure of yesterday, our spirit molds.

A Calendar Stopped in Time

Pages turned, but moments freeze,
Time stands still in a gentle breeze.
Circles drawn in ink of tears,
Each mark holds fragments of our years.

An open window, the world a blur,
Faded photos, a heart's sweet spur.
Yesterday's fragrance fills the air,
In lost tomorrows, we find our care.

Hands of clocks fight against the chain,
Yet in the silence, we remain.
A calendar trapped, with dreams entwined,
In the stillness, we search for what we find.

Flickering Flames of Remembrance

A candle glows in the darkened night,
Casting shadows, a trembling light.
Each flicker tells a story dear,
Of moments shared, of love and fear.

Embers dance, in whispers they breathe,
Reminding us of what we believe.
Memories linger, soft and warm,
In the depths of heart, they take form.

As the fire fades, yet sparks remain,
We hold them close, through joy and pain.
In flickering flames, we find our way,
In remembrance, we choose to stay.

The Silence of Sunset's Farewell

The sky blushes in warm embrace,
As daylight fades without a trace.
Clouds whisper secrets, soft and low,
In twilight's arms, where dreams do flow.

Silence falls like a gentle song,
In every heart, it won't be long.
Taking a breath with each soft sigh,
Kissing the day, we say goodbye.

Stars awaken in the fading light,
Guiding our souls through the night.
In the silence, we find our peace,
As sunset bids a sweet release.

Eloquent Silences of the Heart

In whispers soft like fallen snow,
The heart speaks where no words flow.
A gaze, a touch, a fleeting glance,
In silence blooms a timeless dance.

Beneath the shadows, secrets dwell,
Untold stories weave their spell.
Through echoes of the quiet night,
The heart reveals its hidden light.

Though lips may part and voices fade,
In stillness, love is serenade.
With eloquence beyond the ear,
The silent vows are crystal clear.

In tender moments shared alone,
Each heartbeat marks the love we've sown.
A language forged in sacred trust,
In silence deep, we find what's just.

Balconies of Ancient Dreams

On balconies, the past unfolds,
Where whispered winds our fate once told.
Each dream, a star against the night,
In shadows cast, we find our light.

With echoes of a time gone by,
We breathe the thoughts of those who sigh.
Their laughter lingers, bittersweet,
Among the memories, we compete.

The stones beneath our feet have seen,
The rise and fall of hopes serene.
In every crack, a story lies,
A tapestry 'neath ancient skies.

From lofty heights, we gaze afar,
To distant lands and glowing stars.
Each moment captured, cherished, dreamed,
On balconies where life once gleamed.

The Taste of Memory's Honey

Sweet nectar drips from golden days,
In fragrant fields where laughter plays.
Each memory, a drop divine,
A treasure held in heart's design.

The taste of youth, so rich, so pure,
In every smile, a wistful lure.
With sunlit paths and shadows strong,
In echoes sweet, we hum our song.

Each whispered tale, a honeyed thread,
In woven dreams where we once tread.
From bitter past to future bright,
The taste of love ignites the night.

Through seasons change, the flavors blend,
In memory's jar, we seek to mend.
With every crunch of time that's past,
The taste of honey, true and vast.

Birthdays of a Forgotten Youth

In faded photos, laughter springs,
Each birthday held in tender wings.
Yet time, a thief, has come to call,
And memories, like shadows, fall.

With cake and dreams that once held sway,
In jumbled thoughts, we lost our way.
The echoes of our joy now pale,
As wistful winds begin to wail.

Yet through the haze of yesteryears,
A spark remains beneath the fears.
For every wish and candle's light,
Brings back the whispers of delight.

In hearts we cherish what once was,
The birthdays spent in youth's warm buzz.
Though time may fade the colors bright,
The spirit glows with soft twilight.

The Soliloquy of Days Long Gone

In whispers soft, the shadows creep,
Where laughter danced and memories sleep.
The echoes fade of voices dear,
In sunlit halls, I shed a tear.

Each photograph, a story told,
In fading hues, the past unfolds.
The clock ticks on, a steady beat,
Yet in my heart, the moments meet.

Forgotten paths beneath my feet,
Where dreams and sorrows gently greet.
The world moves fast, but I remain,
A steadfast heart, a lingering pain.

With every dawn, I search in vain,
For echoes long lost to the rain.
Yet in the twilight's gentle glow,
The soliloquy of days will flow.

A Journey through Wistful Winds

The winds they sing of journeys far,
Through valleys deep, beneath each star.
I wander through the twilight haze,
In search of light in wistful days.

Each breeze that whispers in my ear,
Brings tales of joy, and hints of fear.
The trees sway gently, time stands still,
In nature's arms, my soul can thrill.

With every gust, a story flies,
Of laughter lost and heartfelt sighs.
I chase the shadows, feel the sun,
This journey winds, yet I've not run.

The paths may twist, the moments bend,
Yet in the heart, the dreams descend.
In each soft breath, I find my peace,
A journey through the winds, release.

The Tapestry of Tender Moments

In threads of gold the memories weave,
A tapestry of all I believe.
Each color bright, each stitch unique,
In tender moments, love we seek.

The laughter shared, the silent glances,
Every heartbeat, in life's dances.
The cherished times, both near and far,
In woven dreams, we find our star.

With every tear, a thread is spun,
In shadows cast, where we have run.
The fabric strong, though time may fray,
In tender moments, love will stay.

So here I sit, in colors bold,
A tapestry of stories told.
In every thread, there dwells the light,
A canvas rich with lives so bright.

The Traces of Forgotten Love

In echoes faint, the whispers fall,
Of once-bright dreams now shadows crawl.
The traces left by wandering hearts,
In silent corners, where love departs.

Forgotten notes, a tattered page,
In corners dark, a ghostly stage.
The laughter faded, smiles grown thin,
In twilight's hush, the heart gives in.

Yet still I hold the memories near,
The traces linger, soft and clear.
Each sigh and glance, a lingering trace,
Of love once known, a soft embrace.

In quiet moments, I still find,
The traces left, though hearts unwind.
For love, though lost, will e'er reside,
In echoes sweet, where dreams abide.

The Carpet of Forgotten Paths

In the folds of time they lie,
Worn threads of footsteps long gone by.
Whispers dance on woven seams,
Tales of lost hopes and fading dreams.

Each color tells a different tale,
Of laughter shared and hearts so pale.
Underneath the dust they wait,
The stories live, though lost to fate.

A tapestry of what once was,
Every knot a silent cause.
Rekindle flames that flicker low,
In the carpet, paths still grow.

When daylight fades to twilight's glow,
The forgotten winds begin to blow.
In shadows deep, the paths will wind,
Leaving memories intertwined.

Plucking the Strings of the Past

Fingers brush the threads of time,
Strumming softly, in rhythm and rhyme.
Echoes rise from distant shores,
Songs of yesteryear, forever pours.

Memories linger like gentle notes,
Carried on the breeze as it floats.
Each pluck a story, each strum a tear,
Resounding whispers held so dear.

In the silence, the music swells,
Melodies of moments, secrets it tells.
A dance of shadows, burning bright,
In the twilight's tender light.

With every chord, the past awakes,
As dreams emerge from the deep lakes.
In harmony with time, we find,
The strings of the past forever bind.

Echoes Beyond the Horizon

Glistening waves kiss the morning sky,
Whispers of worlds where dreams sigh.
Far beyond where the sun does set,
Echoes calling, we can't forget.

The winds carry tales from afar,
Guiding lost souls like a shining star.
In the twilight where shadows blend,
Voices of the past seem to send.

Ripples dance on the surface wide,
Memories in water, against the tide.
Each pulse reflects the dreams we've lost,
And in their depths, we count the cost.

Beyond the horizon, hope ignites,
With every tale, the heart unites.
In the echoes, we find our song,
A journey begun, where we belong.

A Symphony of Old Footsteps

In alleyways where shadows creep,
Old footsteps linger, secrets keep.
Each echo tells a tale of yore,
A symphony of hearts that bore.

With every click of worn-out shoes,
Histories whisper, love and blues.
The rhythm of time, it sways and bends,
In every corner, the past transcends.

A melody of laughter and tears,
Stirring the echoes of distant years.
The drumbeat of hope in every stride,
In the tapestry of time, we hide.

As twilight weaves its gentle thread,
The footsteps dance where dreams are fed.
A symphony plays, both clear and vast,
In the harmony of shadows cast.

Voices in the Whirlwind of Ages

Whispers dance in swirling air,
Echoes of those who dared.
Stories weave through stormy night,
Guiding souls with ancient light.

Time unfolds its dusky wings,
Carrying tales of forgotten things.
With every gust, a memory calls,
In the tempest, history sprawls.

Fleeting moments swirl around,
In the chaos, truth is found.
Voices rise from shadows' breathe,
Offering wisdom beyond death.

In the tempest, hearts align,
Finding peace in sacred rhyme.
In the whirlwind, we shall stand,
Together in this timeless land.

The Art of Time's Embrace

Time glides softly, a gentle flow,
Holding memories, high and low.
Moments linger, then they fade,
In every heartbeat, love is laid.

Painted skies of twilight's hue,
Framing dreams both old and new.
Time's embrace, a lover's art,
Weaving threads that bind the heart.

Each second whispers tales untold,
Events wrapped in warmth, not cold.
In the stillness, we find grace,
A tender touch in time's embrace.

As seasons shift, we learn to bend,
The ebb and flow, a delicate friend.
With every tick, we find our song,
In time's embrace, we all belong.

Lanterns Lighting the Way Back

Dimly glowing, lanterns sway,
Casting light on paths of gray.
In the darkness, hope ignites,
Guiding footsteps, igniting nights.

Flickering flames like hearts alive,
Illuminating the will to thrive.
One by one, they take their place,
A shared journey, a warm embrace.

Through the shadows, we shall tread,
Following light where fears have fled.
Lanterns high, they lead the way,
Back to love, come what may.

In the stillness, voices blend,
With every flicker, we transcend.
Homeward bound, united, strong,
Lanterns guide us, where we belong.

The Gardens of Shared Laughter

In gardens rich, where joy abides,
Laughter blooms like has no divides.
Petals whisper in the breeze,
Sharing secrets of warm reprieves.

Sunlight dances on each bloom,
Filling hearts with sweet perfume.
Here friendships flourish, roots entwine,
In this haven, spirits shine.

Moments gathered like flowers rare,
Every giggle, love laid bare.
In the gardens, we are free,
Harvesting joy, you and me.

As seasons change, we'll plant anew,
Seeds of laughter, in skies so blue.
In shared gardens, life is bright,
Where laughter lingers, pure delight.

Lanterns in a Lost Midnight

In shadows deep, the lanterns glow,
A flicker bright, where dreams may flow.
They guide the lost through twilight's haze,
With whispers soft of forgotten days.

Each beam a hope, to light the way,
Through silent streets where echoes play.
In stillness held, the night unveils,
A tapestry where silence sails.

Beneath the stars, they dance and sway,
In endless night, where wishes lay.
With every spark, a secret's told,
In lanterns' glow, the heart is bold.

So let them shine, though darkness might,
These lanterns bright in lost midnight.
A beacon true, they hold the flame,
Forevermore, they'll stay the same.

Pebbles from the Path Untaken

Along the way, pebbles tread,
Each step a choice, paths to be led.
Nestled soft in nature's hand,
Stories whispered, unplanned, unscanned.

A single stone, a moment's pause,
Reflecting dreams, and the heart's cause.
Each pebble holds a tale to share,
Of journeys lost, of wild despair.

In twilight's glow, the shadows play,
Reminders of the roads astray.
To pick them up, to ponder why,
The paths not walked make spirits fly.

So gather pebbles, let them gleam,
For in their weight, lies a dream.
With every choice, life's song unwinds,
In each untaken path, the heart finds.

Rustling Leaves of Yesterday

In autumn's breath, the leaves confide,
Rustling soft, like secrets sighed.
Colors mingle in a crisp embrace,
Memories dance with gentle grace.

Each leaf a story, whispered low,
Of summer's warmth and winter's snow.
They twirl and tumble, a playful game,
Rustling leaves, all shadows claim.

Through quiet woods, the echoes roam,
A symphony of where we call home.
The past unfolds in hues so bright,
In rustling whispers of fading light.

So pause awhile, let stillness reign,
Listen close to the leaf's refrain.
For in their movement, tales arise,
Of yesterday held in nature's sighs.

The Scent of Rain on Warm Pavement

After the storm, the air feels sweet,
With raindrops kissing the warming street.
A fragrance blooms in the gentle mist,
The scent of rain, too soft to resist.

Each droplet falls, a soft ballet,
A symphony on pavement's sway.
It mingles with whispers of earth and sky,
A moment caught as the clouds drift by.

In stillness held, the silence reigns,
The scent of rain mingles with chains.
Of memories bright, of laughter free,
In each warm drop, pure ecstasy.

So breathe it in, this sweet refrain,
The scent of rain on warm pavement.
In nature's hug, let your spirit soar,
For in this fragrance, we long for more.

Echoing Footsteps on Dusty Roads

In twilight's glow, the shadows fall,
Footsteps whisper, a haunting call.
Dusty trails where memories roam,
Each step a tale, a journey home.

Beneath the stars, the silence speaks,
Of love once lost, of hope that seeks.
The path winds on, through night so deep,
Echoing dreams that softly creep.

The dusty road beneath my feet,
Holds every joy, embraces defeat.
Each echo tells of days gone by,
In every breath, a silent sigh.

As dawn breaks red, the echoes fade,
But in my heart, those footprints stayed.
A journey long, with stories old,
In every step, a tale retold.

Shattered Frames of Happiness

Once framed in gold, now tarnished glass,
Memories flicker like shadows that pass.
Laughter once held in moments bright,
Now draped in sorrow, cloaked in night.

Each smile a shard that cuts so deep,
Promises made, now lost in sleep.
Fractured dreams in a silent room,
Echo the whispers of impending doom.

Time did weave its cruel design,
Turning joy into a lifeless line.
Frames that held our brightest days,
Now showcase only shades of gray.

Yet in the cracks, a glimmer stays,
Reminders of love in faded arrays.
Though shattered, still the light can gleam,
In pieces lies the heart's lost dream.

The Kaleidoscope of Used-to-Be

Through lenses worn with time and tears,
Past moments dance, surrendering fears.
Colors swirl in a vibrant haze,
Each twist reveals forgotten days.

Fragments bright, like scattered stones,
Whisper softly of love and bones.
In every shift, a story glows,
Of laughter echoed in winter snows.

Shapes of joy and shadows of pain,
Turn the mundane into the arcane.
Life in motion, a painted breeze,
Each glance a memory, a heart that sees.

Yet as the world turns, colors fade,
In the kaleidoscope, dreams are laid.
What once was bright may shift and dim,
Yet hold the hope, let the light brim.

A Tattered Quilt of Longing

Stitched with threads of hope and grace,
Memories woven in every space.
Each patch a story, a tear, a smile,
A tapestry of life's long mile.

Faded corners where dreams reside,
Soft whispers held of love and pride.
Yearnings wrapped in the fabric worn,
Comfort found in the ties once sworn.

Yet frayed at edges, the quilt does weep,
For moments lost and promises deep.
In its embrace, a longing sigh,
For days that danced, for nights gone by.

Though tattered now, the warmth remains,
A shelter from the world's fierce rains.
In every stitch, a piece of my soul,
A quilt of longing that makes me whole.

Remnants of a Sunlit Afternoon

Golden rays filter through trees,
Whispers of time in the breeze.
Shadows dance on the ground,
Echoes of laughter abound.

A blanket sprawled 'neath the sky,
Moments captured, they fly.
A soft sigh, a gentle touch,
In memories, we clutch.

The warmth of the fading light,
Promises held, shining bright.
As the day comes to a close,
Nature in silence bestows.

A fleeting glance of the past,
Sunset, shadows are cast.
Yet in the heart, they remain,
Remnants of joy, no pain.

The Weight of an Old Love Letter

Faded ink on yellowed page,
Words of a once fiery rage.
Promises written with care,
In lonely moments, I stare.

Each line, a story unfolds,
Whispers of love, secrets told.
Softly held in trembling hands,
Echoes of life's shifting sands.

The heartache masked by a smile,
A testament of love's trial.
Bound by paper, but it feels,
As heavy as life's steely reels.

Yet in the folds, hope remains,
Memories wrapped in sweet chains.
Time may fade, yet love's tether,
Holds strong through any weather.

Unraveled Threads of Childhood

In gardens where wildflowers grew,
Dreams and laughter, skies so blue.
Adventures spun on whispered winds,
Secrets shared, where joy begins.

Marbles glinting in sunlight's glow,
Imaginings where stories flow.
Every corner held a quest,
Innocence, the heart's true best.

Crayons scribbled on paper bright,
Worlds created in pure delight.
Days of wonder, nights of bliss,
Moments we truly miss.

Yet in memory's warm embrace,
Childhood holds a sacred space.
Though years may pass, we still find,
Unraveled threads of heart and mind.

When the World Was Simple

Days stretched long with endless play,
In fields where we'd laugh away.
A time when worries stayed small,
Our innocence, encompassing all.

Clouds that changed their shapes so fast,
Dreams of a future yet to cast.
No fears, just wishes on the wind,
With every day, a new begin.

Stars would light the velvet night,
Guiding us with their tender light.
Plans made in whispers and dreams,
Life was brighter than it seems.

In the echo of those days,
Lies a timeless, golden gaze.
When the world was simple and pure,
A sweet memory we endure.

Fragments of Laughter in the Wind

In the breeze, soft giggles play,
Whispers of joy, fleeting and light.
Carried away, they dance and sway,
A melody lost in the fading night.

Echoes of youth in a sunbeam's glow,
Painted on skies, a canvas so wide.
Laughter like petals, a gentle flow,
Drifting through time, our hearts open wide.

Beneath the trees where secrets lay,
We chased the shadows, wild and free.
Fragments of laughter, come what may,
A treasure preserved, just you and me.

In the twilight, memories blend,
The wind carries tales from days of yore.
With every gust, our spirits mend,
Fragments of laughter forever soar.

Cradled by the Ghosts of Our Past

In the twilight, shadows softly creep,
Whispers of stories woven in time.
Echoes of laughter, secrets we keep,
Cradled by memories, reason, and rhyme.

Old photographs in the dusty light,
Fingers trace faces we used to know.
In every heartbeat, a flickering sight,
Ghosts of our past in the undertow.

Lonely corridors, footsteps resound,
Ghostly voices through hallways roam.
In silence, their presence is richly found,
Cradled by shadows, we wander home.

Every sigh tells of love once lost,
Yet in the shadows, we find our peace.
Remembering warmth at a bittersweet cost,
Cradled by ghosts, our worries cease.

When Time Slept in the Garden

Beneath the boughs where daisies grow,
Time once rested, serene and still.
Petals unhurried, a gentle show,
Nature's embrace, a tender thrill.

Morning dew glistens like silver threads,
Each drop a promise, each moment a song.
In the hush of the leaves, a whisper spreads,
When time slept, nothing felt wrong.

Sunlight filtered through emerald leaves,
Sketching dreams upon the ground.
In this haven, the heart believes,
When time slept, joy could be found.

The world stood still, where worries fade,
In a sweet solitude, we breathed, we played.
When time slept in the garden bright,
Love bloomed eternal in golden light.

Chasing Shadows of the Forgotten

In the alleys where memories dwell,
I wander alone, searching for light.
Echoes of laughter, a distant bell,
Chasing shadows into the night.

With every corner, a tale untold,
Whispers of love lost in the rain.
In dusty corners, brave and bold,
Shadows dance, easing the pain.

Moonlight glimmers on cobblestones,
A guide to the stories, so bittersweet.
Chasing shadows that feel like home,
In the silence, our hearts repeat.

Fading moments, like dreams set free,
Each step a heartbeat, a pulse of grace.
Chasing shadows, just you and me,
In the forgotten, we find our place.

Milton Keynes UK
Ingram Content Group UK Ltd.
UKHW021349011224
451618UK00023B/225